JOHN BILLINGTON

Friend of Squanto

JOHN BILLINGTON
Friend of Squanto

By CLYDE ROBERT BULLA

Illustrated by Peter Burchard

New York: THOMAS Y. CROWELL COMPANY

By the Author

To the Sullivans,
Ray, Ruth, Eric,
and Steve

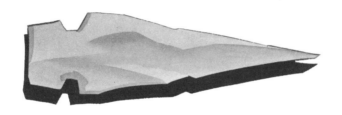

Contents

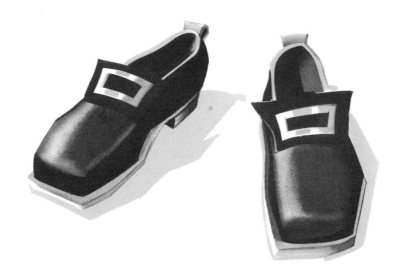

1: John Billington's Shoes

The rain was over and the sun was out. The boys on the *Mayflower* were playing soldier again. Up and down they marched, across the deck of the ship.

"Left, right—left, right!" shouted Giles Hopkins. Giles was one of the older boys. Today he was the captain.

"Here we go under London Bridge!" he said, and he led the way under the big sails of the *Mayflower*.

John Billington marched at the end of the line. He

was one of the younger boys, but he could march as well as any of the others. He knew the right way to hold his wooden musket on his shoulder, and he knew how to keep in step.

Now and then he looked down at his shoes. They were black, with shiny buckles. His father had bought them in London Town just before the *Mayflower* sailed for the New World.

John was proud of his shoes. Every day he rubbed them with a piece of candle to make them shine. They still looked new.

Love Brewster marched beside him. "Big shoes!" he said.

John said nothing.

"Big shoes!" Love said again.

"My father got them big so I could wear them a long time," said John.

"They look like boats," said Love. "They are so big you could sail in them."

"I like them big," said John.

"Left, right!" shouted Giles Hopkins.

Love put his foot down on John's shoe.

"You stop that," said John.

Love put his foot down on John's shoe again. John took his wooden musket in both hands. He brought it down on Love's head. The musket was only a thin piece of wood. It broke in two with a loud crack.

All the boys stopped marching.

"John hit me!" cried Love.

"He stepped on my shoe," said John.

Love's brother Wrestling spoke up. "Love didn't mean to do it."

"Yes, he did," said John.

"John Billington, you're always fighting," said Giles. "You're always making trouble on this ship. You can't play soldier with us any more."

"I don't care," said John.

But he did care. He liked to play soldier.

He went to the rail and looked out at the ocean. The other boys went on playing. They did not ask him to come back and play.

After a while he went below.

A few of the *Mayflower* families had small cabins of their own. The others lived and slept in the long room between decks. John found his mother in the long room. She was sitting by the bunk where John's brother Francis was asleep.

Francis was older than John, but he was not as strong. Whenever the ocean was rough, he was seasick.

"Can Francis play with me now?" asked John.

"Hush!" said Mistress Billington in a whisper.

"Don't make any noise. You'll wake the baby."

Then he saw that his mother held a baby in her arms. It was Mistress Hopkins' baby boy. His name was Oceanus, because he had been born on the *Mayflower* while the ship was on the ocean.

"I'm taking care of Oceanus while his poor mother gets some rest," whispered Mistress Billington.

"Let me hold him," said John.

"You know you're not to hold the baby," said Mistress Billington. "Run along now. Play somewhere else."

Ellen More, Humility Cooper, and Remember Morris were playing on the floor. John watched the three girls. They were playing with their dolls. The dolls were only rags tied together.

"You can't play with us," said Humility.

"Yes, he can, if he wants to," said Ellen.

"I don't want to," said John.

He went to the other side of the room. A young man was sitting there. He was writing in a little book.

"Good day, Master Winslow," said John.

"Good day," said Edward Winslow.

"Every day I see you writing in your book," said John.

"Yes," said Edward Winslow. "I write about the voyage of the *Mayflower*. I tell about the things that happen on the voyage."

"What are you writing today?" asked John.

"Shall I read it to you? Listen." Edward Winslow began to read: " 'November 2, 1620. Today the waves are not so high, and the sun shines. It is 56 days since we sailed from England. With so many men, women, children, and sailors on this ship, there is little room for anyone. We all wish for the sight of land—' "

"Why do you write those things?" asked John. "We know them already."

"Our friends in England may want to know about our voyage," said Edward Winslow. "Some day they may read what I write." He put away his book.

On the deck above they could hear the boys playing soldier.

"Why do you not play with them?" asked Master Winslow.

"They don't want me," said John.

"Have you been fighting again?" asked Master Winslow.

"A little," said John.

Master Winslow shook his head. "Listen to me," he said. "Do you know why we are on our way to America?"

"Yes," said John. "Because we want to live there."

"And why do we want to live there?" said Master Winslow. "I'll tell you, John. Because we want to be free and have a better life than we had at home. But it won't be easy at first. In the New World there will be no one to help us, so we must help one another. We must all stand together, with no fighting among ourselves. Do you understand?"

"Yes, Master Winslow," said John.

"Good. See that you don't forget." Master Winslow got to his feet. "Come, let's go on deck."

Up on deck the boys were still playing soldier. Master Winslow called to Giles Hopkins, "Here is another soldier for you."

Giles frowned.

"He wants to be a good soldier, don't you, John?" said Master Winslow.

"Yes," said John.

"Well—get in line," said Giles.

John began to march at the end of the line. He had no musket, but he was glad to be marching with the others again.

2: *The New World*

There was a week of storms and rain. John and his brother Francis could hear the wind as they lay in their bunk at night. They could hear the *Mayflower* creak and groan.

Francis said one night, "This old ship is going to break in two."

"No, this is a good ship," said John.

Their mother had not yet gone to bed. She came to the bunk. "Go to sleep," she said.

Francis shut his eyes.

"I'm not sleepy," said John. He looked out across the big room. The children on the *Mayflower* were always put to bed early. They were all in bed now. But most of the men and women were still up.

By the light of a candle, Edward Winslow was writing in his book. Old John Carver was reading his Bible. Master Mullins and his wife were reading the Bible, too, and their daughter Priscilla was sewing.

Captain Miles Standish and Master William Bradford were looking at a map.

John saw his father talking with some of the younger men—Tom Tinker, Edward Dotey, John Goodman, and big John Alden. He knew they must be talking about the New World. He wanted to hear what they said.

John said to his mother, "I want to get up and sit with my father."

"It's too cold for you to be running about in your night clothes," she said.

A fire burned on the sand in the iron fire-box.

"I'll keep warm," said John. "I'll sit by the fire."

"I'll warm you with my hand if you get out of that bed," said Mistress Billington.

"Well, if I can't get up, will you bring me a drink?" said John.

She brought him some water in a wooden dipper. "It tastes bad," said John.

"You'll get no better on this ship," said his mother.

"Why does it taste like rotten wood?" asked John.

"Because it's been in an old wooden barrel for the last two months," said Mistress Billington. She sat down by the bunk. She pulled the cover up under John's chin. "Ah, John, do you remember when we had all the water we wanted? Good, sweet water to drink and wash with?"

"Yes, I remember," he said.

"Do you remember the good things we had to eat at your grandma's house?" she asked. "Pies and puddings and apples and plums? Now there's nothing but bread and salt pork and stew with just a bit of meat in it. Ah, it's a hard life."

"Yes, it's a hard life," he said.

"But we'll have good times yet," she said quickly. "Your father and I are young and strong. We'll have good times in the New World."

"When are we going to get there?" asked John.

"I can't say," said his mother. "It might be tomorrow."

"You say that every day," said John. "Tomorrow—tomorrow!"

"What's all the noise here?" said a deep voice. John saw his father by the bed.

"Go to sleep, John," said Mistress Billington.

"Yes, and no more noise!" said his father.

John said no more. He shut his eyes. He lay very still until he went to sleep.

When he woke, it was morning. A long way off someone was shouting. All the people were climbing out of bed. Everyone began to talk at once.

John's mother bent over him. "Wake up!" she said.

"What's the matter?" he asked.

"There's land in sight!" she cried.

John began to shake Francis.

Francis turned over in bed. He was only half awake. "Is the ship going to break in two?" he asked.

"No, there's land in sight," said John. "Get up, Francis. Let's go see!"

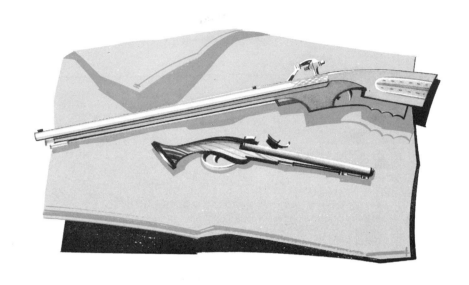

3: *In the Gun-Room*

At first there was not much to see—only a high cliff and some trees.

John Goodman had brought his two dogs on the *Mayflower*. He led them up on deck. They turned their noses to the shore and began to sniff and bark.

"They smell the land!" said Master Goodman.

"I can smell the land, too," said John Billington. "When the wind blows, I can smell grass and trees."

He and Francis were at the rail. Their mother and

father were with them. They watched the shore. They saw the ship run into rough water.

For a while it looked as if they would never reach land. The waves made a roaring sound. They beat and shook the *Mayflower* until it seemed the ship would fall to pieces.

It was night before Captain Jones and the sailors brought the *Mayflower* into safe water.

In the morning they sailed on again. They sailed around a tip of land into a fine, deep harbor. Captain Jones told them they had come to the coast of New England. The tip of land was Cape Cod.

Captain Miles Standish came on deck. He wore a suit of armor. There was a sword at his side, and he carried a musket.

"We cannot all go ashore now," he said. "There may be Indians in the woods, waiting to shoot us full of arrows. Some of us must go first. We must find out if it is safe to land."

He chose the men to go with him. They put out in a small boat and rowed ashore.

John and Francis stood by the rail. They watched the men drag the boat up on the sand.

"When Father goes to shore again, I'm going with him," said John.

"You would just be in the way," said Francis.

"No, I wouldn't," said John. "Master Winslow says the boys and girls have to help, too. I can help Father."

"What can you do?" asked Francis.

"I can fight Indians," said John.

Francis laughed. "No Indian would be afraid of you."

"He would be if I had a musket," said John.

Francis laughed again. "A musket is bigger than you are. You couldn't carry one."

"I wouldn't have to carry it," said John. "I could be a guard. When I saw Indians coming, I could shoot."

"You don't know how to shoot a musket," said Francis.

"I saw Captain Standish one day when he showed the men how."

"But *you* don't know how," Francis said.

"I'll show you!" said John.

He went below. Francis went with him.

They went to the gun-room. Sometimes the door was locked. Today it opened when John gave it a push.

"It's dark in here," he said.

Francis ran away and came back with a lighted candle.

They went into the gun-room. On the floor were muskets rolled up in sail-cloth. There were barrels of gunpowder, too, and boxes of bullets.

"Show me how you fire a musket," said Francis.

John took one of the muskets out of the sail-cloth. He stood it up on the floor.

"You load it first," he said, "like this." He poured some gunpowder down the muzzle. He dropped a bullet on top of the gunpowder. "Then you put some more powder in this pan on the side of the musket— like this. Then you put a match to it—"

Francis was watching. He was holding the candle close.

"Don't get too close," said John.

As he spoke, the powder in the pan caught fire. The gun roared and leaped out of John's hands. He fell to the floor.

He heard Francis shouting, "Get up! Get up!"

He got up. "Run!" said Francis.

They ran out of the gun-room. They ran down a ladder and into the hold in the bottom of the ship.

It was dark in the hold. They felt their way over some water barrels. They lay down behind them.

"I burned my hand," said John.

"Don't talk so loud," said Francis. "We've got to hide."

"I don't want to hide," said John. "I want Mother to put some butter on my hand so it won't hurt."

"If she finds us, she'll give us a beating," said Francis.

"I didn't mean to shoot the musket," said John. "I was just showing you how."

"But you did shoot it," said Francis. "You shot a hole in the side of the gun-room."

"It won't do any good to hide," said John.

"Yes, it will," said Francis. "If we hide long enough, people will start to forget what we did. Then we won't get such a hard beating."

The door of the hold opened. Someone called,

"Come out! Come out at once, you wicked boys!"

John and Francis lay very still.

"If they are down there in the dark, let them stay," said someone else. "It may teach them a lesson."

The door of the hold fell shut.

All the rest of the day and all night they hid in the dark. In the morning big John Alden came down and dragged them out.

"Shame, shame, you wicked boys!" he said. "If the barrels of gunpowder had caught fire, you might have blown up the whole ship."

He dragged them into the big room between decks. Master Billington was there, and Mistress Billington.

Master Billington had a stick in his hand.

"Come here, both of you," he said. He bent the stick back and forth in his hands.

Old John Carver came forward. "Hear me, Master Billington. Remember this is Sunday."

"What of that?" asked Master Billington.

"Would it be right to beat the children on the Lord's day?" said Master Carver.

"They are my children," said Master Billington. "I'll beat them when I like."

But he waited. After a while he put the stick aside.

John and Francis sat on their bunk. Mistress Billington brought their breakfast porridge in two wooden dishes.

John began to sniff. "What is it that smells so good?"

"It's a branch from a juniper tree. We're burning it in the fire-box," said Mistress Billington. "It's some of the juniper the men found yesterday on Cape Cod."

"Did the men have any adventures?" asked Francis.

"No," said his mother. "They saw no Indians, and they say it is safe for us to go ashore tomorrow."

"I want to go," said John.

"Will you let us go?" asked Francis.

Mistress Billington gave them a long look. "I don't know," she said. "After what happened yesterday, I really don't know."

4: A Track in the Woods

Early the next morning the women were on deck, ready to go ashore. They had bundles of clothes to wash.

"Won't it be good to have all our clothes clean again!" said Mistress Hopkins.

"Will we have fresh water to wash them in?" asked Priscilla Mullins.

"Yes, I think so," said Mistress Hopkins.

"I do hope so," said Priscilla. "It's hard to get clothes clean in salt water."

The children were on deck. "We want to go, too," they were saying. "Please, please let us go!"

"It is so long since the children have had their feet on land," said Priscilla. "I think they should go."

Edward Winslow came across the deck. "Captain Standish says the children may go," he said.

The boys and girls set up a shout. John and Francis Billington called to each other, "We're going ashore! We're going ashore!"

"Some of us men will be there, too," said Edward Winslow. "We will stand guard while the women wash the clothes."

"Is there danger?" asked Priscilla.

"We think not," said Edward Winslow. "But if Indians are hiding in the woods, it is well to be ready."

The men put a small boat over the side. The women threw their bundles of clothing into it. They climbed down the ladder into the boat. The children climbed down after them.

John and Francis sat on a bundle of clothes.

"I'll be the first one out," said Francis.

"No, I will," said John.

"Sit still," his mother told him. "Don't hurt your hand again."

"It doesn't hurt now," said John.

He stood up in the boat. As soon as it touched land, he jumped out. Francis jumped out after him.

They slipped in the sand. They both fell down and got up laughing. It was good to feel land under their feet. They began to run, kicking up the sand as they went.

"Stop!" shouted Edward Winslow.

The boys turned back.

"Wait until the guard is ready," said Edward Winslow.

Six men with muskets stood guard at the edge of the woods.

The women found a little pond. They gathered around it and began to wash their clothes.

The children played along the beach. They picked up rocks and shells.

Giles Hopkins began to dig in the sand. "My father

says there are clams here, and clams are good to eat," he said.

Soon the other boys were digging for clams.

John caught a crab. He held it between his thumb and finger so it could not bite him. He ran to show it to the girls.

Humility Cooper began to scream. "Don't let it bite me!"

The girls ran away, and John ran after them.

Priscilla Mullins picked up a stick. "John Billington, you stop that!" she cried.

He laughed, as she started after him. He dropped the crab and ran.

He ran into the woods. When he looked back, he saw that Priscilla had not followed him.

He knew that he should go back to the beach, but he wanted to see what the woods were like. He went a little farther.

He kicked the dead leaves under his feet. He put his hand down to feel the moss on a tree trunk. And there in the soft earth at the foot of the tree he saw a footprint.

He looked down at it. It was not the print of an English shoe.

His father had once told him that Indians wore soft shoes made of animal skins. He knew that this must be the print of an Indian shoe. Not long ago an Indian had stood here.

He began to feel strange. He felt as though

someone might be watching him from behind a tree.

Just then someone called him. "John! John Billington!"

It was his mother's voice.

He ran back to the beach.

"Didn't you hear the men say we must stay together?" she said. "Don't ever go into the woods again by yourself!"

"Mother," he said, "I saw where an Indian stood."

"What?" she said.

Edward Winslow came up. "What are you saying?"

"I saw where an Indian stood," said John. "I saw the print of his foot."

"Where?" asked Edward Winslow.

"In the woods," said John.

Master Winslow made a sign to the other men on guard. "The boy says he saw an Indian track," he said. He asked John, "Can you show us where it is?"

"Yes," said John.

Edward Winslow and Tom Tinker went with him into the woods. They held their muskets ready.

"It was here," said John. "No, it was there."

He looked from one tree to another.

"You don't know where it was, do you?" asked Edward Winslow.

John shook his head.

They went back to the beach. Master Winslow told the other men, "John thought he saw an Indian track, but he can't find it now."

The women went back to washing clothes and hanging them on the bushes to dry. The children began to play again.

Love Brewster asked John, "Why did you say you saw an Indian track?"

"I did see it," said John.

"Why couldn't you show it to the men?" asked Love.

"I couldn't find it," said John.

"Maybe there wasn't any Indian track," said Love.

"There was! There was!" said John, but he knew that no one believed him.

5: *Plymouth Harbor*

Two days later the small boat pulled away from the *Mayflower* again. This time the women and children were left behind.

John and Francis waved to their father as the men rowed away.

"Why couldn't I go, too?" said John. "I could help them cut wood and dig clams."

Mistress Billington was at the rail nearby. "This time they are not going to cut wood or dig clams," she said. "They are looking for a place to build our houses."

"We could build them there on the beach," said John.

"They are looking for a better place," said his mother. "We want a place where the earth is better for growing things. We want to live near a good harbor where ships can come in and out. We want to live near a stream, too, so we can have fresh water all the time."

"Will we have a house all our own?" asked Francis.

"Yes, all our own," she said.

"I hope it has a stone chimney like my grandma's house in London Town," said John. "Will it have a stone chimney, Mother?"

"Ask your father," she said.

"I will," said John, "when he comes back tonight."

But the men did not come back that night or the next. It was not until the end of the third day that the little boat came back to the *Mayflower*.

The men were tired and hungry and cold. In the room between decks they sat by the fire. While they rested and warmed themselves, they told of what they had seen.

"We saw Indians!" said Master Hopkins.

"Did you hear?" said John to Love Brewster. "There *are* Indians in the woods. It *was* an Indian track I saw."

Love said nothing.

John asked his father, "Did you fight the Indians?"

"No," said his father. "There were only five or six of them. When they saw us, they ran into the woods."

"Did you see where they lived?" asked John.

"We saw some of their fields." Master Billington took a handful of seeds out of his pocket. Some were red, some were yellow, and some were blue. "This is Indian corn. We found a basketful and brought it back to the ship."

John tried to chew a grain. It was so hard he could not crack it with his teeth.

"I can't bite it," he said.

"It has to be cooked first, or made into flour," said his father. "But Captain Standish says we must not eat

this. Next year we will plant it and grow corn of our own."

"Did Captain Standish say where we are going to live?" asked Mistress Billington.

"No," said Master Billington. "We found some places, but not the *right* place."

It was hard for them to find the right place. All through the rest of November and part of December they looked up and down Cape Cod.

"We should build our houses here at the end of the Cape," some of them said.

"No," said others, "there are better places."

One morning eighteen men set out in the small boat. It was almost a week before they came back to the *Mayflower*. They were so tired they could hardly pull themselves up the ladder. Their hands and faces were stiff with cold.

Master Billington went below and lay down on his bunk. John and Francis pulled off his shoes. Mistress Billington put a blanket over him.

"Rest now," she said.

"I must talk first," he said. "I have much to tell. We have fought a battle with the Indians."

"Oh, mercy!" cried Mistress Billington.

"We were on Cape Cod. We had camped there all night," he said. "In the morning there was such a shouting and yelling as you never heard in all your life. Indians were coming out of the woods. They were shooting arrows left and right. We let fly at them with our muskets, and they ran away into the woods. The battle was over almost as soon as it had begun, and no one was hurt."

"But you might have been killed!" said Mistress

Billington. "You had done nothing to those Indians. Why did they shoot at you?"

"Captain Standish says they may be angry because we took their corn," said Master Billington. "We didn't stay long enough to find out the reason. We got into our boat and left the place. On Cape Cod Bay the wind and rain caught us, and the boat was almost a wreck."

"Don't tell me any more," cried Mistress Billington. "I can't bear to hear it!"

"The news is not all bad," said Master Billington. "We made camp at a place called Plymouth Bay. The earth there is good for farming. There is a good harbor. A stream of fresh water runs into it."

"Are we going to build our houses there?" asked Mistress Billington.

"I think so," he said. "It's the best place we have found."

"Can we build our house tomorrow?" asked John.

"Not tomorrow," said Master Billington, "but soon, I hope."

6: The Billington House

The *Mayflower* sailed across Cape Cod Bay and into Plymouth harbor. Again the women and children stayed on the ship while the men went ashore.

Mistress Billington told John and Francis, "The men are building a Common House, big enough to hold all the families on the *Mayflower*. When it is done, we will go ashore."

"You said we were going to have a house of our own," said John.

"So we are," said his mother, "but it all takes time."

"Why can't John and I go ashore with the men?" asked Francis.

"Can't you see it is winter now?" said Mistress Billington. "Can't you see how our poor men come back to the ship, sick and half frozen? You would only go and freeze with them."

On a Sunday in January all the *Mayflower* families did go ashore, but only for a little while. Everyone

crowded into the Common House. Master Brewster preached, and they all prayed together. Then they walked through the wind and snow to the boat that took them back to the *Mayflower*.

But two days later the Billingtons went ashore again. This time they went to stay.

At first they lived in the Common House. Mistress Billington helped care for the men who were sick.

The men who were able to work built houses for

their families. John and Francis helped their father build the Billington house. They brought mud from the river to fill the cracks in the sides. They brought sticks and dry grass, and their father tied it into bunches of thatch. He used the thatch to make a roof.

It was a tiny house. There was only one room, and the floor was of dirt.

John liked the house when his mother and father were there. But most of the time they were away.

"While your father and I are well and strong," said Mistress Billington, "we must help care for the sick."

One night John and Francis were alone in the house. They sat close together before the small fireplace. The fire had burned low, and there was no more wood. Their father had not had time to cut wood that day.

"Mother said we must go to bed when the fire burned out," said Francis. "She said we must go to bed to keep warm."

"It's warm in the Common House," said John. "Why can't we go there?"

"Because of the sick people," said Francis. "If we

went there, we might catch the sickness." He went to bed. "You'd better get under the covers before you get cold."

John got under the covers. It was warm there, but he could not sleep. He had had only a little dish of stew for supper. Now he was hungry again.

After a while he got up. He blew on the coals and the fire blazed up. It made a little light in the room.

He looked in the iron pot that hung in the fireplace. There was no stew left.

He went to the door and looked out. He hoped he would see his mother and father coming home.

The moon shone on the snow. Across the little town of Plymouth, lights were shining through oiled-paper windows.

His mother and father were not in sight, but when he saw the lights, he felt better. He did not feel so lonely. He lay down again and went to sleep.

When he woke, there was candlelight in the room. Mother and Father were there. He could hear them as they spoke softly together.

"Captain Standish's wife died today," said Mother. "The little More boy, too."

"There may be others tomorrow," said Father.

"It is no wonder so many of our people are sick," she said. "There is not enough good food for all, and our houses let in the cold."

"We saw the smoke of Indian fires again today," said Father.

"Do you think the Indians are coming nearer?" she asked.

"Yes. They are watching us," he said. "They fear our muskets and cannon. But our people are sick and weak. How can we fight back if the Indians make war on us?"

"If I must, I can fire a musket," she said.

John said to himself, "I can fire a musket, too." And he lay there, thinking how he would fire it—how he would put the musket up through the window and stand ready if the Indians came.

Men began to come out of the Common House. They stood in a circle around the Indian.

"He can't get away now," said Francis. "Let's run."

They ran home.

"Mother!" they shouted.

But she was not there. They found her in front of the Common House with all the other people of Plymouth. They were looking at the Indian. They were trying to hear what he said.

"He knows some English words," said Edward Winslow. "He says he learned them from English hunters who came here once."

"Did you hear the first word he spoke to us?" asked John Alden. "He said, 'Welcome!'"

Ellen More and Humility Cooper were hiding behind Mistress Hopkins.

"Did you see the Indian?" asked Humility, as John and Francis went past.

"His name is Samoset," said Ellen.

"He looked at me," whispered Humility, "and I felt cold all over!"

7: "Welcome"

It was a long and terrible winter. Before the coming of spring, only half the people who had landed at Plymouth were still alive.

On the first warm day they all came out of their houses. They turned their faces to the sun as if they could not get enough of it.

John and Francis started down the street. Their mother called them back. "Where are you going?"

"To the Common House," said John.

"You can't go there," she said. "The men are having a meeting."

"What is the meeting for?" asked John.

"Ask your father," she said.

"I know what the meeting is for," said Francis, as he and John walked away. "I heard Governor Carver talking yesterday. He said Captain Standish was going to call the men together to make an army to fight the Indians."

"It won't be a very big army," said John.

"No," said Francis, "but we have guns and cannon. The Indians have nothing but bows and arrows and knives and spears."

They walked along the river. At the edge of the woods they saw a little black dog with a bushy tail.

"There is one of Master Goodman's dogs," said John.

They whistled and called, but the dog would not come near.

"He is a wild dog now," said John.

"Yes," said Francis. "No one fed him or took care

of him after Master Goodman died last wi

"Now he's running away," said John. "He's of something."

"I hear something in the woods," said F "Hide!"

He hid behind a rock. He pulled John down him.

They looked around the side of the rock. A came out of the woods. His hair was long and His skin was the color of a copper kettle. He had and arrow in his hand.

He walked past the place where the boys wer ing. He did not see them.

"It's an Indian!" whispered Francis.

John stood up. "We've got to run and tell body."

"He'll see us if we do," said Francis. "Look, he goes, right into town!"

The Indian was walking down the street of outh. At the Common House he stopped. He s to go inside.

7: *"Welcome"*

It was a long and terrible winter. Before the coming of spring, only half the people who had landed at Plymouth were still alive.

On the first warm day they all came out of their houses. They turned their faces to the sun as if they could not get enough of it.

John and Francis started down the street. Their mother called them back. "Where are you going?"

"To the Common House," said John.

"You can't go there," she said. "The men are having a meeting."

"What is the meeting for?" asked John.

"Ask your father," she said.

"I know what the meeting is for," said Francis, as he and John walked away. "I heard Governor Carver talking yesterday. He said Captain Standish was going to call the men together to make an army to fight the Indians."

"It won't be a very big army," said John.

"No," said Francis, "but we have guns and cannon. The Indians have nothing but bows and arrows and knives and spears."

They walked along the river. At the edge of the woods they saw a little black dog with a bushy tail.

"There is one of Master Goodman's dogs," said John.

They whistled and called, but the dog would not come near.

"He is a wild dog now," said John.

"Yes," said Francis. "No one fed him or took care

of him after Master Goodman died last winter."

"Now he's running away," said John. "He's afraid of something."

"I hear something in the woods," said Francis. "Hide!"

He hid behind a rock. He pulled John down beside him.

They looked around the side of the rock. A man came out of the woods. His hair was long and black. His skin was the color of a copper kettle. He had a bow and arrow in his hand.

He walked past the place where the boys were hiding. He did not see them.

"It's an Indian!" whispered Francis.

John stood up. "We've got to run and tell everybody."

"He'll see us if we do," said Francis. "Look, there he goes, right into town!"

The Indian was walking down the street of Plymouth. At the Common House he stopped. He started to go inside.

Men began to come out of the Common House. They stood in a circle around the Indian.

"He can't get away now," said Francis. "Let's run."

They ran home.

"Mother!" they shouted.

But she was not there. They found her in front of the Common House with all the other people of Plymouth. They were looking at the Indian. They were trying to hear what he said.

"He knows some English words," said Edward Winslow. "He says he learned them from English hunters who came here once."

"Did you hear the first word he spoke to us?" asked John Alden. "He said, 'Welcome!' "

Ellen More and Humility Cooper were hiding behind Mistress Hopkins.

"Did you see the Indian?" asked Humility, as John and Francis went past.

"His name is Samoset," said Ellen.

"He looked at me," whispered Humility, "and I felt cold all over!"

Master Billington left the circle of men. He said to his wife, "I don't like this."

"What is wrong?" she asked. "Surely one Indian can do no harm."

"It's plain to me," said Master Billington, "that the other Indians sent this man to spy on us. They want to know how many men we have and how strong we are."

"And then the Indians will make war on us?" asked John.

"I think that is what they mean to do," said Master Billington. "But if they do make war, they will find us ready."

And he led his wife and children up the street and into their own house.

8: Squanto

Samoset slept that night in the house of Master Hopkins. In the morning he started off into the woods.

The Billingtons watched him go.

"See how he walks," said Mistress Billington, "light as a cat."

"They all walk like cats," said Master Billington, "and some night they will come creeping up like cats and—"

"Stop!" said Mistress Billington. "You must not

make the children afraid." She spoke in a low voice, but John heard her.

"I'm not afraid," he said.

"And neither am I," said his mother. "For all we know, the Indians may be our friends."

There were others in Plymouth who thought as she did.

A week after Samoset's visit, some of the men were talking in the Common House. John Billington was there with his father.

"Let us give more time to digging the fields and planting our crops," said Master Hopkins. "Let us not give so much time to making ready for war. It was the Indians on Cape Cod who shot their arrows at us. The Indians who live to the west of Plymouth may be our friends."

"They may be friends, and they may not be," said Miles Standish. "Until we are sure, we will keep our cannon and muskets ready."

Governor Carver spoke. "Some of us must plant the crops while others guard our village."

A shout went up outside. A voice cried, "Indians!"

"To arms!" said Captain Standish. He took up his musket and ran outside. The other men followed him.

Down the street of Plymouth came two Indians. One was Samoset. The other was a younger man, tall and straight and slim.

"Welcome!" said Samoset.

"Friends!" called the other Indian. "We are friends!"

Captain Standish went to meet them. "Where do you come from?" he asked the younger Indian. "How did you learn to speak English?"

"In England I live many years," said the Indian.

"Then you must be the Indian I've heard about," said Captain Standish. "Is your name Squanto?"

"I am Squanto, yes, yes!" said the man. He pointed across the river to Strawberry Hill. "Chief Massasoit waits there. He will talk to your chief."

"Tell your chief to come here," said Captain Standish, "and we will talk to him."

John Billington did not wait to hear any more. He ran home.

"Mother," he said, "the Indians are here."

"I know," she said. "Look."

John looked across the river. He saw Indians standing on top of Strawberry Hill. There were more than he could count. He could see the beads and feathers they wore and he could see the paint on their faces.

While John and his mother watched, they saw a band of Indians start down the hill. One Indian walked ahead. He wore many beads and feathers.

"He must be the chief," said John.

"Come," said Mistress Billington. "Let us go to the Common House. If there is any danger, we will be near your father and the other men."

They waited in front of the Common House with the other people of Plymouth.

The Indians came down the street.

"Shall we take them into the Common House?" asked Edward Winslow.

"No, no!" said Miles Standish. "Our muskets and swords are there."

"Let the chief and our governor meet in my house," said Master Hopkins.

So Chief Massasoit and Governor Carver went into the Hopkins house. Squanto went with them.

They were inside a long time. When they came out, they were smiling.

Governor Carver said, "We have talked together in friendship. Squanto knows both the English and the Indian language, and he has helped us understand each other. Chief Massasoit and his tribe will be our friends, and we will be theirs. When the Indians come to visit us, they will leave their bows and arrows at home. When we visit them, we will leave our muskets at home. Now we must be happy together. The women will prepare a feast, and this will be a day of feasting."

The women looked at one another.

"So we must prepare a feast," said Mistress Billington.

"Yes," said Priscilla Mullins, "when we have not enough food for ourselves."

But they brought biscuits and cheese and fish. They set the food before the hungry Indians.

It was a day of feasting. In the morning the Indians told the white men good-by. They waded across the river.

But one Indian stayed behind. That Indian was Squanto.

John Billington stood on the river bank and looked
at him. All the other Indians wore paint on their faces,
but Squanto's face was not painted.

John had thought that all Indians were cruel and
fierce, but this Indian looked kind.

Samoset called back across the river, "Are you coming?"

Squanto shook his head. "I stay," he said.

And John was glad that Squanto was going to stay.

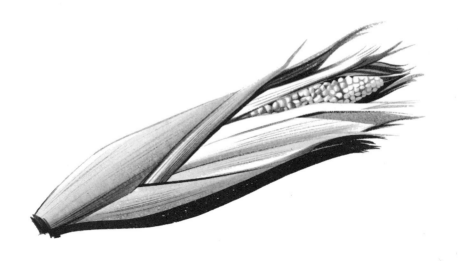

9: Squanto's Story

Before long all the people of Plymouth were glad Squanto had stayed. He showed them how to plant Indian corn. He taught them to make grass nets for catching fish. He showed them the best places to hunt and fish. After Squanto came, there was more food on the Plymouth tables than ever before.

He liked to be near the children. He showed the girls how to weave grass mats. He taught the boys to make bows and arrows.

John Billington followed him everywhere.

One day he and Squanto were on the shore together. All the other people of Plymouth were there, too. They were watching the *Mayflower* sail away.

"Why your ship sail away?" asked Squanto.

"The ship doesn't belong to us. It belongs to some people in England," said John. "Now the captain has to take it back."

"Once I go to England," said Squanto. "I go on big ship."

"How did you get on the ship?" asked John.

"White men come here," said Squanto. "Take me on ship. All the way to London I go. Long time I live in London. White men very good to me there."

"How did you get back home?" asked John.

Squanto told him. While the *Mayflower* sailed out of sight, he told his story. "Captain John Smith bring me back to Massachusetts. I start home to see my mother—see my father."

"Did you surprise them?" asked John.

"I not see them," said Squanto. "Before I get to my

village, some white men catch me. They tie me and take me away on ship. They take other Indians on ship. That bad man Captain Hunt take us to Spain."

"What for?" asked John.

"He sell us for slaves," said Squanto.

John looked at Squanto. "Were you—were you a slave?"

"No, no," said Squanto. "The good men of the church, they save me. They send me to England. White men bring me again to Massachusetts."

"Did you go to your village?" asked John. "Did you see your mother and father?"

Squanto looked out across the water. He said, "*Mayflower* gone."

"Yes, it's gone," said John. He asked again, "When you came back from England, did you see your mother and father?"

Squanto did not answer. He went away toward the river.

Now that the *Mayflower* was gone, all the people went back to their houses.

Some of them were sad.

"Now we are here alone," said Mistress Hopkins.

"But the days are warm now," said Edward Winslow. "We have roofs over our heads, and we know better how to live in the New World."

John walked beside him, back to the Common House.

"Squanto told me he had been to England twice," he said. "I asked him if he saw his mother and father when he came home, and he wouldn't tell me. Why wouldn't he tell me, Master Winslow?"

"I don't think he wants to talk about it," said Edward Winslow. "It's a sad story. Samoset told it to some of us on the day he brought Squanto here."

"What is the story?" asked John.

"He never saw his mother and father again," said Master Winslow. "When he came home, his village was gone. All his people were gone, too."

"Where?" asked John.

"A sickness had come and taken all his tribe," said Edward Winslow. "He went away to the village of

Massasoit, but he was not happy there. He had lived with white men so long that it was hard for him to live as an Indian again. One day he heard that the *Mayflower* had come and Englishmen were living where his village used to be."

"Is this where Squanto's village used to be?" asked John. "Where Plymouth is now?"

"Yes," said Edward Winslow. "Squanto says he has come back home. He says we are his people now."

After that, John always tried to be kind to Squanto. He went with him everywhere.

"Sleep in our house," he said.

And sometimes Squanto did sleep in the Billington house, but most of the time he slept in the Common House alone.

10: Trouble

A week after the *Mayflower* sailed, the sickness came again. This time it took Governor Carver.

"He was a good man," the people said, and everyone was sad.

"But our work must go on," said the new governor, Master Bradford. "We have fields to tend and more houses to build. We must make ready for the year to come."

All through the long winter, John Billington had thought there would never be any good times in

Plymouth. But when the days grew warm and the children could be outside, they began to play again.

Sometimes they played among the rocks along the shore. Sometimes they played by the edge of the woods.

On the river bank was an old tree half covered with grapevines.

"We make swing," said Squanto. "I show you."

He cut one of the vines free so that it swung from a branch above.

"Make good swing—yes, yes!" he said. He caught the vine in both hands and swung back and forth.

"Let me try," said Giles Hopkins. He ran and caught the vine in his hands. "Look! You can swing a long way!"

The other boys took turns. The girls came to watch them.

"I want to swing," said Humility Cooper.

"You don't know how," said John.

"Yes, I do." She took hold of the vine, but she did not know how to swing herself back and forth.

"See? You can't swing," said John.

"I could if somebody swung me," said Humility. "Swing me, John."

"Hold up your feet," he said. He gave her a push, then another and another.

"Look at me!" said Humility. She swung out over the river. She looked down and saw the water below. The sight made her dizzy.

"Stop!" she cried. She let go of the vine and fell into the river.

The water was not deep, and she was not hurt, but the fall had frightened her. "Help!" she cried.

Giles Hopkins pulled her out. Still she kept crying, "Help, help!" as she ran toward home.

Mistress Brewster called to her, "What is it, child?"

"John Billington was pushing me!" said Humility.

Soon the story went up and down the street that John had pushed Humility into the river.

Mistress Billington broke a stick off a plum tree and went out to look for John. She found him by the river with the other boys.

"Did you push Humility?" she asked.

"Yes," said John.

"Then you're a bad boy," she said, and she whipped him with the plum stick. She led him home and put him to bed for the rest of the day.

John was angry. That evening at supper he would not speak to anyone.

"What's the matter with John?" asked his father.

"I had to whip him," said Mistress Billington. "He pushed poor little Humility into the river."

"She was on the grapevine swing when he pushed her," said Francis. "He pushed her out over the river and she fell in."

"That's just as bad," said Mistress Billington. "It was a foolish thing to do, swinging the little girl out over the water."

"Yes, it was a foolish thing." Master Billington said to John, "After this, try to keep out of trouble."

John did try. But before many days he was in trouble again.

He and Francis were playing by the cornfield. They

were playing a game they had made up. It was called
Big Brown Bear.

Francis was the big brown bear. He went through
the bushes, looking for John. When he found him,
John jumped up and ran.

Francis tried to catch him. He growled as he ran.
"I'm the big brown bear, and I'm going to get you!"

"No!" shouted John. "You can't catch me!"

He ran toward home. He ran around the house,
with Francis close behind him.

There was a pile of wood beside the house. John climbed to the top of it. From the pile of wood he jumped to the roof.

Mistress Billington was in the house. She was peeling onions for supper, when she heard a noise above her head. She saw a foot and leg come through the roof.

She dropped the onions and ran outside.

"John Billington!" she cried. "What are you doing up there?"

"The big brown bear is after me," he said.

"*Where?*" she cried.

"There!" said John.

"I'm the big brown bear," said Francis.

"Oh, so it's one of your jokes!" Mistress Billington pulled John down off the house. "I'll teach you to poke holes in our roof!"

She turned him over her knee and spanked him.

All along the street, people looked at one another and shook their heads. John Billington was getting spanked again, they said. John Billington was the worst boy in Plymouth!

11: *Two Indians*

John told his mother the next day, "I'm going away to live with the Indians."

"If you do," she said, "the Indians will soon send you back."

He told Squanto, too, "I'm going to live with the Indians."

"No, no," said Squanto. "Indians not live same as white men. House not the same. Food and clothes not the same. No, no, you not like." He put his hand on

John's head. "You not leave good home. Not leave mother, father, brother."

"Maybe I will," said John.

"Some Indians, they not friend to white men," said Squanto. "You know that?"

"Yes, I know it," said John. "On Cape Cod they shot arrows at my father and the other men."

"Yes, yes," said Squanto. "You not go."

So John stayed. There was work for all, and he worked hard that summer. He carried water from the river. He caught fish and cleaned them. He helped keep the weeds out of the fields.

"You see," said Master Billington. "You can be a good boy if you try."

But one day John was in trouble again.

He and Wrestling Brewster were playing leapfrog near the cornfield. John jumped over Wrestling's back. He landed in the cornfield and broke off a stalk of corn.

Master Hopkins was working in the field. "Oh, wicked, wicked!" he cried. "A good ear of corn would have grown from that stalk."

Master Billington was working at the other end of the field. He came running to see what John had done.

"For shame!" he said. "We work hard to grow this corn, and you tramp it under your feet."

He picked up the broken stalk. He whipped John across the legs with it.

It did not hurt much. What hurt most was that the other boys and girls were there to see.

John turned and ran. He ran into the woods, farther than he had ever been before.

He looked back and saw that no one had followed him. Then he stopped running. He walked among the trees.

It was cool there. Birds were singing. He watched a red squirrel jump from limb to limb. In a little while he felt better.

He found a small stream running through the woods. He lay down and drank from it. He liked the feel of the grass beneath him. It was softer than a bed. He lay there and listened to the wind among the leaves, and his eyes closed.

When he opened his eyes, the woods looked strange. There were shadows all about him. The sunlight was gone. He knew that he had been asleep.

He got up and began to walk very fast so that he would get home before dark.

The woods grew darker. He stopped and tried to look about him. He did not know where he was. He did not know the way back to Plymouth.

Once, long ago, he had been lost in the streets of London. He had not been much afraid then. He was not much afraid now. He knew that someone would come looking for him.

He climbed a tree where he would be safe from bears and wolves. He sat on a wide branch and laid his head against the tree trunk.

Soon he would see a light moving through the trees, he thought. That would mean that someone had come to find him.

He waited and watched for a long time. The only light he saw was the light of the moon coming up over the trees.

In the morning he slid down out of the tree. He had slept part of the night, but he still felt sleepy. He shook his head and rubbed his eyes to wake himself up.

He started off through the woods. He hoped he was

walking toward Plymouth. Once he thought he heard someone behind him. He looked back. There was no one in sight.

He walked a little farther and looked back again. This time he saw an Indian standing very still beside a tree.

John walked faster. He could hear the Indian walking behind him.

The next time he looked back, there were two Indians. They were Indians he had never seen before. They did not have friendly faces. He did not think they belonged to Chief Massasoit's tribe.

They came close to him. One of them made a sign for him to walk between them.

"Are you taking me back to Plymouth?" asked John.

But he saw that the men did not know what he was saying.

One of them spoke some words in the Indian language. He took hold of John's arm, and John walked along between the two Indians.

12: The Indian Village

They walked a long way. The Indians took such long steps that it was hard for John to keep up.

They came to the sea. When John saw the shore, he knew where he was. If he walked north along the shore, he would come to Plymouth.

He pointed toward home. "That way," he said.

The men did not answer. One of them pulled a canoe out of the bushes and slid it into the water. The other Indian set John in the canoe.

"The other way," said John, as they paddled away from the shore.

The Indians kept paddling toward the south.

"No!" John pointed back toward Plymouth.

One of the Indians spoke in a sharp voice. John said no more.

He thought that the men must be Cape Cod Indians because they were headed for Cape Cod. He knew that some of the Indians there were not friendly to white men.

He began to plan how he could get away. When they landed, he would jump out of the canoe, he thought. He would run into the woods before the men could catch him.

But when the Indians paddled to shore, they were out of the canoe before he was.

They walked into the woods and down a trail.

The trail led to an Indian village. Some of the houses were made of grass mats. Others were made of the bark of trees.

Before one of the houses a woman was putting sticks

on a big fire. Children were playing in the dust nearby.

One of the Indians with John gave a shout. The woman looked up. The children stopped playing. They all looked at John.

People came out of the houses and out of the woods. Everyone stood still and looked at John.

Then they all began to talk at once. John saw that they were excited. He thought he must be the first white boy they had ever seen.

Some of the men came close to him. They touched his hair. They felt the cloth of his shirt.

John saw a man eating a piece of meat. He remembered that he had had nothing to eat since yesterday. He looked at the man and kept looking at him. At last someone gave John a piece of deer meat. It was dry and a little burnt, but it tasted good to him. He stood and ate it, while all the Indians watched.

John slept that night in one of the houses. In the morning the two Indians who had brought him to the village took him away. They followed a trail that led far up into Cape Cod.

Late in the day they came to another village.

From all over the village people came to look at John. A man came out of the largest house. He wore deerskins and many strings of beads. His mouth was straight, as if he never smiled. Everyone made way for him. John was sure that he was the chief.

The two Indians with John began to talk. The chief listened and nodded his head.

He spoke to John.

"I don't know what you are saying," said John.

They stood looking at each other. Then the chief went back into his house.

That night John went to bed in one of the Indian houses. His bed was a mat on the floor. Others came in and lay down on the floor. One of them was a boy no larger than John.

All over the village the Indians sang themselves to sleep. The noise kept John awake. His clothes kept him awake, too. It was hard for him to sleep in his clothes as the Indians did. His shoes were heavy, and his stockings were hot.

Late at night, John sat up on the mat. He took off his shoes and stockings and put them beside him. Soon afterward he was asleep.

When he woke in the morning, he heard people walking and talking outside the house. He smelled food cooking.

He lay there and tried to think what to do. At first he had been afraid of the Indians, but now he was not afraid. They were not friendly, but he did not think they were going to harm him.

He looked about him. He was alone in the house. He felt for his shoes and stockings. His stockings were there on the floor beside him. His shoes were gone.

He ran to the doorway. "Where are my shoes?" he cried. He had forgotten that no one in the village knew his language. "Who took my shoes?"

He saw the Indian boy who had slept near him in the house. The boy was wearing John's shoes!

John ran out of the house. The Indian boy saw him and started to run. He tripped on the shoes and fell. Before he could get up, John was sitting on him and pulling off his shoes.

The Indian boy was frightened. He jumped up. He ran away, shouting and waving his hands.

John picked up his shoes. He saw that all the people in the village had been watching. They were smiling. Some of the men were even laughing, showing their teeth and shaking their shoulders. The chief was laughing the hardest of all.

He sat down outside his house and made a sign for John to come to him. He patted the mat beside him.

"Thank you," said John, and he sat down beside the chief and put on his shoes.

13: Chief Aspinet

Every day John tried to tell the Indians that he wanted to go home. They listened and shook their heads. He could not make them understand.

He lived in the house of the chief. Many people came to see him. They looked at his clothes. They looked at his hands and face. An old woman tried to look at his teeth.

The people were kind to him, but he did not like to live in the Indian village. He had no one to talk with. He did not know the games the children played. He missed his mother and father and Francis.

Once he walked out of the village. He wanted to find the seashore. From there he thought he could find his way to Plymouth. But a strong young Indian came after him and carried him back to the village.

He did not know how he could ever get home again.

He had been with the Indians almost a week, when he saw that there was excitement in the village. The chief and the Indian braves talked together. All the people kept looking toward the woods.

The women and children went into their houses. A woman led John into her house. She hung a mat over the door.

He sat beside her in the dark. When he tried to look out, she pulled him back.

He heard a man talking outside. He was talking in the Indian language, but John knew the voice.

Before the woman could stop him, he kicked the

mat aside. He went running through the doorway.

"Squanto!" he cried.

Squanto was there, talking with the chief.

"John!" he said. "We look and look, and I find you!"

"Take me home," said John.

"Yes, yes," said Squanto. He and the chief talked in the Indian language. Then Squanto told John, "Chief Aspinet say he like white boy. He say white boy stay."

"I don't want to stay," said John.

Again Squanto and the chief talked. Squanto said to John, "Boat on shore. I go. I tell men I find you."

"Aren't you going to take me with you?" asked John.

"Chief say he bring you to boat," said Squanto.

"Maybe he won't," said John.

"He bring you—yes, yes."

Squanto went away. Chief Aspinet and his braves made ready to take John to the boat. They painted their faces red and blue. They put feathers in their hair and beads about their necks.

They put feathers in John's hair, too. They hung long strings of beads about his neck.

It was evening when they left the village. Two tall braves took John on their shoulders. Chief Aspinet walked beside them. The other braves walked behind.

They came to the shore. John saw the boat waiting. His father was in the boat. Squanto and Edward Winslow were there, too, and Master Hopkins and Governor Bradford.

John wanted to run to the boat. He tried to get down, but the Indians held him fast. They waded into the water and set John down in the boat.

Chief Aspinet made a long speech. He gave Squanto an Indian knife.

"Chief say knife for white men," said Squanto.

"Tell him we thank him," said Governor Bradford, "and we have a present for the chief."

He gave Chief Aspinet an English knife and a copper chain.

Then Squanto and Edward Winslow pushed the boat away from the shore. They raised the sails.

Master Hopkins looked at John. "Do you know the trouble you have made us? We had to give up our work to look for you."

John waited for his father to scold him. But Master Billington said nothing. He only held John tightly between his knees as the boat sailed away.

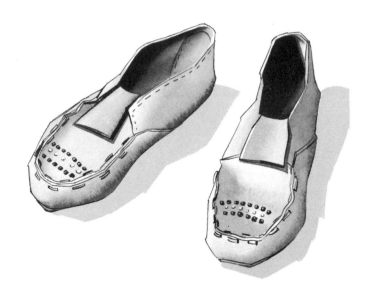

14: Thanksgiving

Not long after John came home, the first cold days of fall came to Plymouth. Then the days turned warm again, and it was Indian Summer. The sky and sea were a clear, bright blue. The trees were red and gold and brown.

The people of Plymouth said to one another, "This is the best time of the year."

The men picked the Indian corn. There was a good crop.

"Let the winter come," said Master Billington. "We have good, strong houses and enough to eat."

"There is much to be thankful for," said Governor Bradford. "Let us have a holiday in which to give thanks. Let us ask our Indian friends to join us in a feast of thanksgiving."

Squanto went into the woods. He spoke to all the Indians he met and asked them to come to the feast.

The day before Thanksgiving, some of the men went hunting. They brought back wild ducks, wild geese, and a deer.

On Thanksgiving morning the women were up early, cooking the game the men had brought. The men set up tables near the Common House.

Long before the feast was ready, Chief Massasoit was there. With him were ninety of his braves. They had brought five more deer and a dozen wild turkeys.

For two days the people feasted together. They played games and sang songs.

By the third day most of the food had been eaten. Edward Winslow went up the river to look for more turkeys. He was back almost at once. He came running down the street of Plymouth. He found Captain Standish in the Common House.

"There are Indians in the woods!" said Edward Winslow.

"There are Indians here in Plymouth, too," said Captain Standish.

"But these are strange Indians," said Master Winslow. "I fear they mean us no good. I fear they came here to catch us while we are feasting and fall upon us with their bows and arrows."

"I shall call our men together," said Captain Standish. "Tell the women and children to come to the Common House."

The children were playing at the edge of the woods. Master Winslow started toward them. Then he cried, "It is too late!"

The Indians had come out of the woods.

"They have caught one of our boys!" said Captain Standish.

"It is young John Billington," said Master Winslow.

"Quick—to arms!" cried Miles Standish. "They must not get away."

But the Indians were not trying to get away. They came straight toward Plymouth.

They walked in a long line. At the head of the line was a chief. Beside him were two tall braves, and on their shoulders sat John Billington.

They came down the street of Plymouth.

Mistress Billington saw them and cried out, "John!"

"Be quiet," said Master Billington. "They have done him no harm."

Squanto went to meet the Indians. "Chief Aspinet," he said. "Chief Aspinet come to Plymouth—yes, yes!"

He and the chief talked for a while. Captain Standish and Governor Bradford came near. Squanto told them, "The chief know you have feast. He come to feast. He say Indians on Cape Cod be friends to white men."

"Tell him he is welcome," said Governor Bradford.

"Aspinet say he come to see young white chief," said Squanto.

"Young white chief?" said Captain Standish. "Does he mean John Billington?"

"Yes, I think he does," said Governor Bradford.

"I want to get down," said John.

The governor took him down off the Indians' shoulders. He made a speech. "We can all be thankful for what has happened this day," he said. "The Indian tribes on Cape Cod lived in fear of us. We lived in fear of them. Then this boy went among them as a friend. Young John Billington has led the way to friendship between us."

The white men gave the Indians presents. They gave them knives and mirrors and hats and a compass. The Indians gave the white men animal skins. There was a present for John, too. It was a pair of Indian moccasins.

The moccasins were made of soft deerskin. There were blue and white beads on the toes.

John thanked Chief Aspinet. He said to his mother and father, "I needed new shoes. See how worn my old ones are?"

"This has been a hard year for shoes," said Mistress Billington.

"And a hard year for people," said Master Billington.

"But we are young and strong, and we are still together," said Mistress Billington. "Let us be thankful."